D1556932

ENGINEERING SUPER STRUCTURES

SKYSCRAPERS

PAIGE V. POLINSKY

Consulting Editor, Diane Craig, M.A./Reading Specialist

Sandcastle

An Imprint of Abdo Publishing
abdopublishing.com

abdopublishing.com

Published by Abdo Publishing, a division of ABDO, PO Box 398166, Minneapolis, Minnesota 55439. Copyright © 2018 by Abdo Consulting Group, Inc. International copyrights reserved in all countries. No part of this book may be reproduced in any form without written permission from the publisher. SandCastle™ is a trademark and logo of Abdo Publishing.

Printed in the United States of America, North Mankato, Minnesota

062017
092017

THIS BOOK CONTAINS
RECYCLED MATERIALS

Design: Kelly Doudna, Mighty Media, Inc.
Production: Mighty Media, Inc.
Editor: Rebecca Felix
Cover Photographs: Mighty Media, Inc.; Shutterstock
Interior Photographs: Library of Congress, Shutterstock

Publisher's Cataloging-in-Publication Data

Names: Polinsky, Paige V., author.
Title: Skyscrapers / by Paige V. Polinsky.
Description: Minneapolis, MN : Abdo Publishing, 2018. | Series: Engineering super structures.
Identifiers: LCCN 2016962889 | ISBN 9781532111051 (lib. bdg.) | ISBN 9781680788907 (ebook)
Subjects: LCSH: Skyscrapers--Juvenile literature. | Skyscrapers--Design and construction--Juvenile literature. | Structural engineering--Juvenile literature.
Classification: DDC 690--dc23
LC record available at http://lccn.loc.gov/2016962889

SandCastle™ Level: Fluent

SandCastle™ books are created by a team of professional educators, reading specialists, and content developers around five essential components—phonemic awareness, phonics, vocabulary, text comprehension, and fluency—to assist young readers as they develop reading skills and strategies and increase their general knowledge. All books are written, reviewed, and leveled for guided reading, early reading intervention, and Accelerated Reader™ programs for use in shared, guided, and independent reading and writing activities to support a balanced approach to literacy instruction. The SandCastle™ series has four levels that correspond to early literacy development. The levels are provided to help teachers and parents select appropriate books for young readers.

EMERGING • BEGINNING • TRANSITIONAL • FLUENT

CONTENTS

About Skyscrapers

Skyscrapers are tall buildings.

They are built in cities
around the world.

The first skyscraper was built in 1885. It had a **steel** frame. This made it very strong.

Cities can be crowded.

There is often little room
to spare. City planners must
use space **efficiently**.

Skyscrapers are very big. But they take up little ground space.

Instead, they are very tall. Some
have more than 150 floors!

Skyscrapers are used for
many things.

Some **contain** apartments. Hundreds of people can live in one building!

Other skyscrapers hold hotels and stores. Many **contain** offices.

The Empire State Building holds offices. It is a famous skyscraper in New York City.

It is 1,454 feet
(443 m) tall.

It takes careful planning to build a skyscraper. The **foundation** must be secure.

If it is not, the building could
collapse.

Earthquakes can **damage** tall buildings. So can strong winds.

But **engineers** build
skyscrapers solid
and sturdy.

Think About It

What is the tallest building you
have been in? Was it a skyscraper?

GLOSSARY

collapse – to fall down suddenly.

contain – to consist of or include.

damage – to cause harm or ruin.

earthquake – when the ground shakes or trembles.

efficient – able to do something without wasting time, money, or energy.

engineer - someone who is trained to design and build structures such as machines, cars, or roads.

foundation – a structure that supports a building from underneath.

steel - a strong, hard metal made from iron.